CLASH
of CULTURES

Prehistory – 1638

★★ *The Drama of* AMERICAN HISTORY ★★

CLASH
of CULTURES

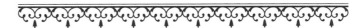

Prehistory −1638

Christopher Collier
James Lincoln Collier

BENCHMARK **B**OOKS

MARSHALL CAVENDISH
NEW YORK

ACKNOWLEDGMENT: The authors wish to thank Neal Salisbury, Professor of History, Smith College, for his careful reading of the text of this volume of The Drama of American History and his thoughtful and useful comments. This work has been much improved by Professor Salisbury's notes. The authors are deeply in his debt but, of course, assume full responsibility for the substance of the work, including any errors that may appear.

Photo research by James Lincoln Collier..

COVER PHOTO: *Jamestown-Yorktown Educational Trust*

PICTURE CREDITS: The photographs in this book are used by permission and through the courtesy of: © *Plimoth Plantation/Ted Curtin*: 13 (top). *Jamestown-Yorktown Educational Trust*: page 13 (bottom), 15 (top), 15 (bottom), 17 (all), 31, 32, 33 (top, *detail*), 33 (bottom, *detail*), 49 (*detail*), 54. © *Plimoth Plantation/Gary Andrashko*: 16. *National Museum of the American Indian*: 19 (all), 22 (left), 22 (right), 23, 25 (top), 25 (bottom). *Corbis-Bettmann*: 35, 36, 41, 42, 45, 46, 47, 53, 55, 59, 63 (left), 63 (right), 64, 65, 71, 73, 77, 81. *Plimoth Plantation*: 37.

AUTHORS' NOTE: The human beings who first peopled what we now call the Americas have traditionally been called *Indians,* because the first Europeans who landed in the Americas thought they had reached India. The term *Indians* is therefore not very accurate, and other terms have been used: *Amerinds,* and more recently, *Native Americans.* The Indians had no collective term for themselves. Today, most of them refer to themselves as Indians, and we will use that term here, while understanding that it is not very accurate.

Benchmark Books
Marshall Cavendish Corporation
99 White Plains Road
Tarrytown, New York 10591-9001

© 1998 Christopher Collier and James Lincoln Collier

Library of Congress Cataloging-in-Publication Data

Collier, Christopher, date
Clash of cultures, prehistory–1638/
by Christopher Collier, James Lincoln Collier.
p. cm. - (The drama of American History)
Includes bibliographical references and index.
ISBN 0-7614-0436-8 (lib. bdg.)
1. Indians of North America—History—Juvenile literature. 2. United States—History—Colonial period, ca. 1600-1775—Juvenile literature. 3. Culture conflict—North America—Juvenile literature. 4. Indians of North America—First contact with Europeans—Juvenile Literature.
I. Collier, James Lincoln, date. II. Title.
III. Series: Collier, Christopher, date Drama of American history
E77.4.C65 1998   96-31859
970.00497—dc20   CIP

Printed in the United States of America

3 5 6 4

CONTENTS

PREFACE

Over many years of both teaching and writing for students at all levels, from grammar school to graduate school, it has been borne in on us that many, if not most, American history textbooks suffer from trying to include everything of any moment in the history of the nation. Students become lost in a swamp of factual information, and as a consequence lose track of how those facts fit together, and why they are significant and relevant to the world today.

In this series, our effort has been to strip the vast amount of available detail down to a central core. Our aim is to draw in bold strokes, providing enough information, but no more than is necessary, to bring out the basic themes of the American story, and what they mean to us now. We believe that it is surely more important for students to grasp the underlying concepts and ideas that emerge from the movement of history, than to memorize an array of facts and figures.

The difference between this series and many standard texts lies in what has been left out. We are convinced that students will better remember the important themes if they are not buried under a heap of names, dates, and places.

In this sense, our primary goal is what might be called citizenship education. We think it is critically important for America as a nation and Americans as individuals to understand the origins and workings of the public institutions which are central to American society. We have asked ourselves again and again what is most important for citizens of our democracy to know so they can most effectively make the system work for them and the nation. For this reason, we have focused on political and institutional history, leaving social and cultural history less well developed.

This series is divided into volumes that move chronologically through the American story. Each is built around a single topic, such as the Pilgrims, the Constitutional Convention, or immigration. Each volume has been written so that it can stand alone, for students who wish to research a given topic. As a consequence, in many cases material from previous volumes is repeated, usually in abbreviated form, to set the topic in its historical context. That is to say, students of the Constitutional Convention must be given some idea of relations with England, and why the Revolution was fought, even though the material was covered in detail in a previous volume. Readers should find that each volume tells an entire story that can be read with or without reference to other volumes.

Despite our belief that it is of the first importance to outline sharply basic concepts and generalizations, we have not neglected the great dramas of American history. The stories that will hold the attention of students are here, and we believe they will help the concepts they illustrate to stick in their minds. We think, for example, that knowing of Abraham Baldwin's brave and dramatic decision to vote with the small states at the Constitutional Convention will bring alive the Connecticut Compromise, out of which grew the American Senate.

Each of these volumes has been read by esteemed specialists in its particular topic; we have benefited from their comments.

CHAPTER I

North American Lives

O ne of the great themes in the history of human life is the clash-
ing of cultures. Everywhere, at all times, groups of people with
different ways of doing things, different ideas about themselves
and the world around them, have been in conflict. This is as true today as
it was as far back as we can see in human history. Such clashes of culture
do not inevitably lead to killing and war; sometimes they are settled
peaceably. But unfortunately, killing is a frequent result of the conflict
between different cultural groups.

The history of what is now the United States began with such a cultural conflict: the dramatic and long drawn-out battle between Europeans
and Indians for control of the continent of North America. And there is
no doubt that the battle was one of the crucial events in human history,
for it changed the state of life on earth forever.

The human beings who first peopled what we now call the Americas
have traditionally been called *Indians*, because the first Europeans who
landed in the Americas thought they had reached India. The term *Indians*
is therefore not very accurate, and other terms have been used: *Amerinds*,
and more recently, *Native Americans*. The Indians had no term for them-

selves, as they thought they were all the human beings that there were. Today most of them refer to themselves as Indians, and we will use that term here, while understanding that it is not very accurate.

They had originally come from the area of Asia loosely known as Siberia. Due to fluctuations in climate, at various times over the past forty thousand years the seas receded, opening a strip of land across the Bering Strait between Siberia and Alaska. People living in Siberia, along with a number of animals, drifted across this land bridge, possibly as early as forty thousand years ago, but certainly by twenty thousand years ago. These people were Stone Age People, who used tools of stone, bone, and wood, crude by modern standards, but good enough for killing and butchering big game, like the mammoths who shared the land with them. Although these people could slaughter big game, they were what are called hunting-and-gathering people, who ate mostly small animals and such eggs, roots, berries, nuts, and seeds as they could collect in their wanderings. They lived in crude shelters made of skins or brush over frames of wood, and they wandered in small bands from one base camp to the next as the seasons changed. In time they worked their way down the Pacific Coast into South America and across North America to the Atlantic Ocean.

By about seven thousand years ago some of these people were becoming farmers, learning how to grow and improve seeds, roots, and other vegetables. Particularly important to them was maize, what we call corn today, although the ears were much smaller than the modern ones. But farming did not take over entirely. Even as late as the 1500s, when the Europeans were first exploring North America, many groups of Indians did little or no farming. Some groups on the Western plains had so many buffalo (correctly called bison) available they had no need of growing things—especially after Europeans had introduced horses into America. And groups in the Northeast, from Maine up into Canada, did not have a climate warm enough for agriculture. On the other hand, groups like

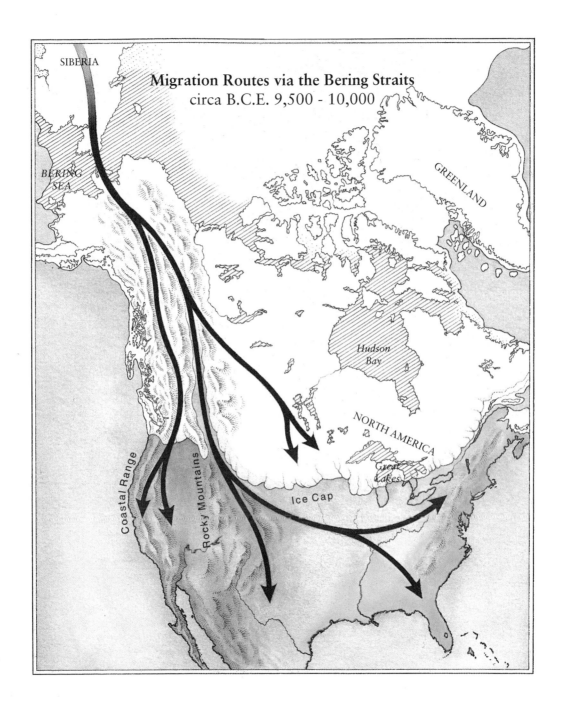

Migration Routes via the Bering Straits
circa B.C.E. 9,500 - 10,000

SIBERIA

BERING
SEA

GREENLAND

Hudson
Bay

NORTH AMERICA

Great
Lakes

Coastal Range

Rocky Mountains

Ice Cap

the Pueblo Indians of the Southwest were avid farmers and based their economy on corn. Then there were what are called mixed economies, which combined farming with hunting and gathering. By the time the Europeans reached North America, the peoples who inhabited the land still had one foot in the Stone Age, but they were moving into a more complex way of life.

Historians are not sure how many Indians lived in North America when the Europeans arrived: The best guesses put it between five and ten million. But some estimates actually run as high as a hundred million for all of America, North, Central, and South. Some areas, like the deserts of the Southwest or the icy tundras of the Far North, were sparsely settled; but lands of abundance, like the Northwest or the eastern coastal plains were filled with large and small villages scattered up and down the coast.

Given the great differences in environment, it is not surprising that Indians in one place lived quite differently from those in another. In the Northwest, the areas we now call Washington and British Columbia, they were a people of wealth who carved those famous forty-foot totem poles and took huge canoes to sea to hunt creatures of the sea—large and small. In the Far North were the people we call Eskimo, who managed to get along in a very harsh climate, hunting for seals and spending the coldest months in domelike igloos made of ice. In the Southwest the Zuni, Hopi, and other groups built pueblos of clay bricks and grew corn and other crops.

The people of North America spoke some five hundred different languages and many more dialects of these languages. Each group had its own religion, its own myths and legends, its own ideas about the afterlife. Thus, when we talk about "Indians" we must understand that we are looking at a patchwork quilt of cultures varying dramatically in size and shape from one another. All told, these millions of Indians lived in cultures far more varied than did the Europeans who first saw America in the 1500s.

Where birch trees were plentiful, Indians built fine, light canoes of birch bark over wooden frames. In most areas they made dugout canoes, by carefully burning away the inside wood and scraping out the charcoal a bit at a time.

Indians liked to settle where rivers met the seas, for here there would always be excellent fishing. With nets like these stretched across the rivers, they could catch great quantities of fish during the annual spawning runs up the rivers.

There are around the United States several historical "theme parks" in which old towns and villages have been carefully restored or reconstructed according to the most reliable historical research. Among the best-known are Plimouth Plantation, which replicates the original Plymouth settlement; Williamsburg, Virginia, which exemplifies a colonial town of the eighteenth century; and Jamestown, which like Plimouth is a replication of the original settlement.

These reconstructions feature people dressed in costumes of the era engaging in various activities the way they would have been done at the time. Many of the pictures in this book are such recreations. They have been worked out by historians who specialize in these periods, and are soundly based. However, it should be borne in mind that these are reconstructions. Undoubtedly, the clothing of the time would have often been worn and patched, the tools mended, the streets frequently muddy or filled with dust.

Nonetheless, these recreations can give us an excellent idea of how people in America's colonial era lived and worked.

Yet these Indians did have certain ways in common. For one thing, most, if not all, of these varied peoples believed the world was inhabited by invisible spirits that were all around them. The sky had its spirit; so did the trees, the stones, the rivers, the earth itself. All of these spirits had to be respected, for they could do humans good or ill. It was particularly important to hunters to placate the spirits of the animals they killed with rituals. The spirits of their own dead had to be respected and worshiped in various ways, for they might have the power to help or harm their descendants. This world of the spirits was very real and alive to the Indians.

Another commonality was that armed conflict was a routine, if not necessarily constant, part of Indian life. "Braves," as they were accurately termed, were prepared for battle from boyhood and felt pressure to

(above) The dwellings of eastern Indians were usually made of a pole framework covered with skins, bark, or woven mats, as is the case here. One Indian is grinding corn in a tall log mortar. The man at the right is wearing a European shirt, which he probably obtained by trade.

(left) Indian women did most of the house construction. Here one is weaving a mat that could be used to cover the frame of a dwelling.

prove themselves valorous in battle. The death of a brother or uncle had to be avenged; even a minor insult might trigger a battle. But Indians were not always feuding with people around them, for sometimes they formed alliances to hunt together or make war on yet another tribe. Indeed, reciprocity—mutual exchange—was at the center of Indian life, so that war was often seen as one kind of exchange; but one that could be avoided by gift giving by both sides. Nonetheless, Indian tribes, groups, and neighboring villages saw one another as potential rivals; inevitably, fighting flamed up from time to time.

It is important for us to understand that the sort of warfare conducted by the Indians was very different from that of the Europeans. Indians' wars were usually small-scale affairs, frequently just a hit-and-run raid on one village by warriors from another. A few men might be killed, a few prisoners taken, possibly some corn stolen. The idea was not to wipe out

Indian men were expected to fight in the village's battles, and boys were trained at an early age to handle bows and axes. This warrior carries a bow and a carefully carved war club.

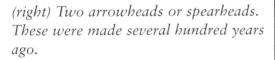

(top left) Indians had little metal, and made many weapons of stone. This a spearhead or arrowhead found in southeastern Virginia. It was probably made in about 5000 B.C.

(top right) A stone ax head with a groove where it could be fastened to a handle. This was made about 2500 B.C.

(right) Two arrowheads or spearheads. These were made several hundred years ago.

the other village, or even, many times, to take over its land. Often the cause of a battle was to avenge a slight, a theft, or even a murder. But very frequently, fighting could be avoided altogether if one group offered the other a symbol of submission, like the gift of corn or furs. For the Indians, war was a kind of deadly athletic contest arranged to take the minimum of lives.

It was a sport, however, with a very unpleasant side to it. Most Indians, especially the males, were trained from childhood to endure pain of any kind, no matter how terrible, without whimpering. In many tribes boys had to go through very painful ceremonies in order to pass into manhood. They might be beaten with sticks; they might be forced to drink poisons that would make them very sick for days; they might be sent off to live in the woods by themselves for weeks at a time. Learning to suffer pain was useful to the Indians, for the males often had to endure hardships in war and the hunt.

Given this concern for pain, it is not surprising that many Indian groups had rituals of torture. This was especially true of the Iroquois of the Eastern woodlands. Prisoners of war were sometimes tortured to death in the cruelest of ways. Their joints might be broken one after the next; they might be roasted slowly, a bit at a time, first one foot, then the other, then the hands. Prisoners were not always tortured, and not every Indian culture engaged in it, but it happened often enough that Indians were taught songs of defiance to sing at their captors as they were going through their agonizing deaths.

The Indians' willingness to endure great pain in manhood ceremonies, the hunt, war, and during times of hardship suggest that tribal law meant a great deal to them. They did not think so much about their individual "rights" as they did about the interests of the tribe. Indeed, they could hardly think about themselves as separate from the tribe: They were one and the same. But when it came down to human authority, it was another story. Indians did not take orders from anybody readily, and as a consequence chiefs had to rule by persuasion, prestige won in battle, or wisdom, rather than force. Alliances of Indian villages or tribes often fell apart quickly, if one member tried to assert authority over the other.

The word *tribe* is the one we usually use when talking about Indian groups, but we need to be cautious in using it. After his family, the basic loyalty of an Indian was to his village or band. These varied considerably in size. In the Eastern woodlands, where the English first began to settle, villages could be as small as a score of dwellings housing as few as a hundred people. Many villages contained a hundred or more dwellings with

(top left) A basketry hat with woven scenes of hunters in canoes chasing whales. This is from the Alaska area and was made in the eighteenth century.

(top right) This gorget was made from a conch shell and was hung around the neck as armor or simply for decoration. The human figure probably had some sort of mythic significance.

(right) These amazing ducks were used for decoys. They were made about 200 A.D., which indicates how sophisticated Indian culture had become by that time.

several hundred people living in them. There were even some villages with as many as three thousand inhabitants. Generally speaking, the size of a village depended on the availability of food. The reason the Indians of the Eastern seaboard were so thickly settled was the richness of the land and water around them. There was good soil for growing corn; a sea full of cod, oysters, and clams; a forest full of deer, bear, and other animals. On the other hand, Indians scratching a living from shallow desert soil might live in small bands of a dozen or so, spread thinly to share the sparse resources of the area.

Village life appeared to be like that of most people everywhere, built around the nuclear family—father, mother, and children. Frequently, closely related families felt special bonds to one another and formed subgroups. In some villages each family had its own dwelling, but in many there were larger dwellings in which related families lived together. But kinship could divide villages, too, as disgruntled individuals or families left to join relations in other villages or tribes.

There were among the Indians no kingdoms or nations in the European sense. Nonetheless, villages were tied together in clusters that spoke the same language, worshiped more or less the same spirits, got their food in the same way, and followed the same sort of customs in marriage, death, war, and illness. These groups of villages are what we often, for shorthand, call tribes. People from several such villages might intermarry. In some cases people who were not getting along well in their own village would transfer to another one. Such villages often saw one another as rivals, competing for the best fishing spots on the lake or the richest cornfields. But they were also natural allies who might band together for mass hunts or to fight other groups. They might even join in sports. In one such game each village tried to carry a ball into the rival village several miles away. Players on each side would bet large amounts in fur, knives, or other goods on the outcome.

The villages usually worked out agreements among themselves about their rights to certain areas for planting, hunting, and fishing. These agreements were often complex, and a lot of the scrapping between villages was caused by competing claims to this or that piece of ground. However, the Indians did not think of themselves as "owning" an area of woods with its deer, or a lake with its fish, in the way Europeans owned land. In a sense, the land owned itself—or at least its spirit did: The Indians only had *rights to use* the land for hunting, planting, and such.

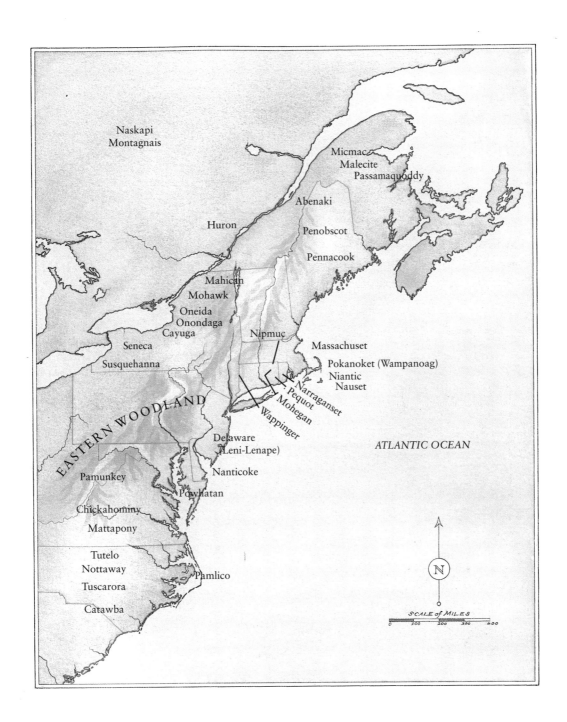

Naskapi
Montagnais

Micmac
Malecite
Passamaquoddy

Huron

Abenaki

Penobscot

Pennacook

Mahican
Mohawk
Oneida
Onondaga
Cayuga

Nipmuc

Massachuset

Seneca

Pokanoket (Wampanoag)
Niantic
Nauset

Susquehanna

Narraganset
Pequot
Mohegan
Wappinger

EASTERN WOODLAND

Delaware
(Leni-Lenape)

ATLANTIC OCEAN

Pamunkey

Nanticoke

Powhatan

Chickahominy

Mattapony

Tutelo
Nottaway

Pamlico

Tuscarora

Catawba

N

SCALE of MILES

0   100   200   300   400

In fact, the Indians had an entirely different idea of wealth from the Europeans. It may seem very strange to us today, but the Indians were not much interested in acquiring things that they could not use. What was the use in owning three knives, four pots, five fur robes, when you only needed one? Extra goods were only a nuisance to take care of and cart along when the Indians traveled or moved the village.

For Indians, wealth beyond what they could use immediately was only of value for trade, as tribute to powerful chiefs, or as gifts of friendship to seal alliances. The exchanging of gifts of fur robes, baskets of corn, or tools was an important part of Indian life. Powerful chiefs who acquired wealth usually distributed it among their subchiefs and allies.

(left) Many American Indians used pottery vessels for storage and cooking and often decorated them with intricate designs. This bowl, made between 1375 and 1475, was found in an abandoned Zuñi village in New Mexico. The parrot design is still used by a Zuñi clan today.

(right) This duck bowl, carved from stone by an Indian artist using only stone tools, was found in Alabama. It was made sometime between 1300 A.D. and 1500 A.D.

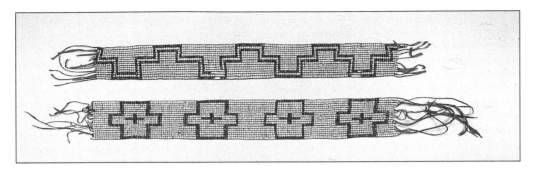

Wampum beads were cut from seashells and often were sewed into belts. Wampum belts were valued by Indians and were used for trading or to symbolize agreements and treaties. These belts were made in the eighteenth century and are about three feet long.

This Indian attitude toward acquiring possessions—the accumulation of wealth—was part and parcel of their feeling that nobody should do any more work than they had to. They would—and did—work very hard when it was necessary: Indian women spent many hours tending their gardens, caring for their children, skinning animals, and making the fur and skin into robes and shirts; hunting parties of males might spend exhausting days tracking deer through the forests. But once they had acquired enough food to hold them for a while, they stopped to enjoy themselves, getting up sports and games, singing and dancing, telling stories, or just loafing in the sun.

What the Indians did value was the physical world around them. They were not environmentalists in our sense: They sometimes overcut the forests, killed more bison than they could use by driving them over cliffs, and as we shall eventually see, when they found they could trade beaver skins for metal knives and hatchets, they hunted beaver ruthlessly.

Nonetheless, to the Indians the natural world was not simply a playground, a place to visit on vacations. Their lives depended on it, and they took their environment very seriously. They knew it was not wise to casually violate the spirits of the deer, the fish, the woods, or the rivers. They viewed the birch trees, the salmon, and the bison almost as people whom they would not injure or destroy for no reason. For example, when the Micmac, a group living in eastern Canada, killed a bear, they would make a speech to its spirit, apologizing for having killed it. The bear carcass was brought into a dwelling through a special door. The bones of bear, martin, moose, or beaver were never just slung to the dogs but were disposed of ritually. They always were careful to treat with respect the living things in their world that kept them alive and healthy.

And they were healthy. Some groups did not do as well as others, of course, and even the most successful groups had times of hunger. But the Indians of the Northeast were taller on average than the Europeans who found them, and they suffered from far fewer of the diseases that were common in Europe, a fact that would prove of immense importance. Moreover, the Indians had developed a very effective pharmacy of herbal medicines made of leaves, grasses, berries, and roots. Some of these curatives were useless, as is often the case with folk medicine, but many of them have been recognized by modern scientists as effective.

Another aspect of Indian life was the indulgence shown to children. Shortly after birth, mothers strapped their children onto a specially shaped board. Thus tied up, the baby could be hung from the mother's back as she walked out to the cornfield, hung from a branch in the breezes, or laid in the shade to sleep as the mother weeded. As the baby grew it was released from the cradleboard and allowed to play.

Of course, even young children were expected to do a share of the work, helping to gather nuts, pick berries, or hoe around the corn hills. In general, they began the tasks they would do as adults quite early, the boys learning to make arrows and shoot at targets, the girls learning, for instance, how to plant and how to cure deerskins. But while children had their tasks, they were not subjected to harsh discipline. When they misbehaved they were not whipped, but gently reproved.

The Europeans who first made contact with the Indians tended to see

This pendant was made of a shell and bits of turquoise and jet about 900–1250 A.D. and was used as jewelry. It was found in New Mexico.

them as savages living rough, even brutish, lives. The Indians had no cattle, no spacious houses, no tables, chairs, clocks, or books. But the fact is that the Indians had developed for themselves a way of life that was comfortable and ample. They ate well, although there were occasions of hunger brought on by drought, storms, or the disruptions of warfare. Their dwellings, if smoky and crowded, were warm and comfortable enough. They enjoyed a great deal of leisure time to sing, dance, and play games. There was always the possibility of adventure—of heightened intensity—in the hunt, in war, in the playing out of natural rivalries. And they lived with a deep sense of belonging to the natural world with its swing of seasons, a part of the grand scheme of things. It was not a life suited to the European taste; and perhaps it would not be to ours today. But in some ways it was a life that fit human nature better than the more structured life of the Europeans.

This effigy jar was probably meant to suggest the head of a dead person, possibly someone who was killed in war and decapitated. It was found in Kentucky and dates from about 1300–1500 A.D.

CHAPTER II

Algonquians and Europeans in the Sixteenth Century

We have been looking at Indian life as it was generally lived across North America. But Indian lifestyles there varied even more widely than did lifestyles across Europe. It must be remembered that there were always variations—groups that avoided war when they could, families who were not kind to their children, tribes that did not torture their captives, and lifestyles ranging from that of the Hopi in their pueblos in the southwest to the Eskimo in their igloos in the extreme north.

We should now look at the specific Indian culture that greeted the Europeans when they first began landing in North America. The earliest efforts to establish outposts were made by the Spanish and French in Florida and along the Gulf of Mexico in the 1500s. But our attention turns now to English settlements on the East Coast, especially the region from the southern border of what is now North Carolina up into Newfoundland, and we need to take a closer look at the Indians who dwelt there.

The group that in the main occupied the lands along the Atlantic were called the Algonquian. They ranged along the Atlantic coast from North

Carolina up to and across Canada to the western plains. Some of the Algonquian tribes have left their names on the land: Massachusetts, Narragansett, Nauset, Montauk. Like most Indians, they believed in the world of spirits and the underlying unity of the natural world. They usually built their settlements along the rivers that flowed east out of the Allegheny Mountains into the Atlantic, most frequently at the mouths of rivers, like the Saco in Maine; the Charles, which flows into Boston Bay; and the Housatonic, Thames, and Connecticut, which flow into Long Island Sound. A particularly important water system was in the Chesapeake Bay area, where the Delaware, Susquehanna, Patuxent, Potomac, Rappahannock, James, and smaller rivers flow into the sea.

The mouths of rivers were very rich in food. In the ocean were vast schools of fish, especially cod. Clams, oysters, crabs, and lobsters could be collected almost without effort along the beaches. In the springtime, saltwater fish like shad and salmon swarmed up the rivers to breed and at times were so thick they could almost be scooped out in baskets. A short distance inland, the woods were full of deer, bear, beaver, squirrel, muskrat, and a dozen other sorts of game. Strawberries grew in abandoned garden plots, and trees produced wild plums, walnuts, hickory nuts, and more. Medicinal herbs were everywhere.

Most important, this well-watered land in a temperate climate was well-suited for agriculture. Indian women grew enough corn, beans, pumpkins, Jerusalem artichokes, and squash to provide at least half, and perhaps two-thirds, of the Algonquian diet, except in Maine and further north, where the growing season was too short for much agriculture. Tribes there depended on hunting, fishing, gathering, and some corn obtained through trade with Indians further south. On the whole, the Algonquian lived on a rich and fertile land, which provided them with a comfortable life.

Their gardening style was simple, but it worked. Kernels of corn would be saved over the winter and planted three or four in a low mound, or hill.

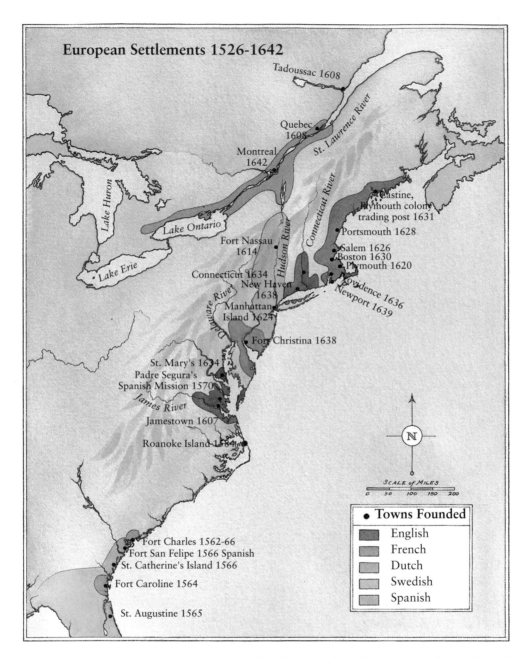

European Settlements 1526-1642

Tadoussac 1608

Quebec 1608

Montreal 1642

St. Lawrence River

Lake Huron

Lake Ontario

Lake Erie

Fort Nassau 1614

Connecticut 1634

New Haven 1638

Manhattan Island 1624

Hudson River

Connecticut River

Castine, Plymouth colony trading post 1631

Portsmouth 1628

Salem 1626
Boston 1630
Plymouth 1620

Providence 1636
Newport 1639

Delaware River

Fort Christina 1638

St. Mary's 1634
Padre Segura's Spanish Mission 1570

James River

Jamestown 1607

Roanoke Island 1584

N

SCALE of MILES
0   50   100   150   200

● **Towns Founded**

	English
	French
	Dutch
	Swedish
	Spanish

Fort Charles 1562-66
Fort San Felipe 1566 Spanish
St. Catherine's Island 1566

Fort Caroline 1564

St. Augustine 1565

Beans, like the kidney bean we are familiar with today, were planted in the hills as well. Between the hills the women would plant pumpkins and squash. The whole system worked together: As the cornstalks rose, the bean vines would twine around them, climbing to the sun. The broad pumpkin and squash leaves would cover the soil, keeping it moist and free from weeds. Nonetheless, Algonquian women and children spent a great deal of time weeding their gardens. We often think of the Northeast Indians as living in forests, but because they grew so much of their food, a lot of the country was open farmland.

Algonquian cooking was surprisingly varied. Meat and fish were frequently boiled in clay pots, sometimes with corn and various nuts, beans, and vegetables to make a rich stew. Meat, fish, and clams could also be roasted on flat stones set over the coals, or directly on the coals themselves. Corn was ground into flour and baked into bread, to which berries or nuts might be added. The kernels could also be boiled whole; unripe green corn was often treated this way. Algonquian women had hundreds of recipes to work from.

As a consequence of this abundance, the Algonquian were populous. The land along the sea, especially at the river mouths, was thickly settled. The Europeans who first visited the area were startled to see villages and open fields stretching for miles along the coast in many places. Some of these villages were surrounded by stockades, but most were not. Some of the Algonquian lived in longhouses which contained several families, but mostly they built smaller dwellings for individual families. Poles were sunk into the ground, bent together at the tops, and lashed. This framework was covered with skins, sheets of bark, or mats woven of the cattail reeds growing in swampy areas along the coast.

These Indians would also trim back growth around grapevines to let the sun shine on the fruit. They routinely burnt off the undergrowth in their woodlands, usually in the spring and fall. The fires killed off a lot of harmful insects and even bacteria; allowed useful grasses and herbs to reappear each spring; and left the ground under the trees clear, which let hunters see deer at a distance and opened paths for the flight of their arrows.

The Algonquian were a relatively settled people. In the spring a village customarily went off to a spot where shad or salmon were swarming.

The Engravings of Theodor de Bry

In 1585 Walter Raleigh got permission from Elizabeth I to explore the New World in search of places to establish an English colony. He sent along on the expedition a scientist named Thomas Hariot and a painter, John White. White made a number of fine watercolors of the Indians and the scenery of the Carolina area where the expedition landed.

Upon returning to England, Hariot, in order to attract people to the new land, wrote an enthusiastic description of what was then known as Virginia. In those days watercolors like the ones John White had painted could not be reproduced in a book. Instead an engraver named Theodor de Bry was asked to make engravings, which could be reproduced. De Bry copied the White paintings quite accurately, although not perfectly. Later on, other people made less successful engravings of the John White pictures, which were published in various places in Europe.

These engravings of the White watercolors, especially the early ones by de Bry, were critical in forming European opinion of North America and the Indians who lived there. With all their faults, they remain the best images we have—aside from the White watercolors themselves—of Indian life before the intrusion of Europeans. At an unknown date some of the engravings were tinted by hand.

They would spend some weeks there, perhaps joined by other villages, peaceably fishing together, even getting up sports and games between rival villages. By late summer they would move back to their sheltered inland quarters to get ready for the harvest season. In the fall they might trek off to a good deer-hunting ground, where the men would hunt and the women would skin and butcher the slaughtered animals. Eventually, after eight, ten, or twelve years, the whole village would relocate, due to dwindling fertility of the soil or a growing shortage of nearby firewood. The women would rebuild the lodgings and put in new gardens. Life

This de Bry engraving from the John White paintings was originally captioned "An Aged Man in his Winter Clothes." It is from the 1588 publication of Hariot's book on Virginia.

would continue as before, and back in their abandoned village the forest would gradually return, creeping into their fields and dwelling sites.

These, then, were the people who inhabited the Atlantic coast of North America in the late 1500s, a people with a distinct, settled, and workable culture that was, nonetheless, slowly evolving, as most cultures do. Through the latter years of the 1500s they would increasingly be visited by strange peoples who appeared suddenly out of the waters to the east, a people with different languages, odd clothing, curious ways of doing things, and novel ideas about the world. Who were they?

The area of the world we call Europe was occupied by modern human beings, probably arriving from Africa or the Near East, about thirty-five thousand years ago. They were hunters and gatherers, nomads who wandered around a series of base camps as the seasons shifted—in a word, very similar to the Indians who first came into the Americas. As was the case with the Indians, the European culture evolved. Perhaps seven thousand years ago the agricultural revolution arrived in Europe and people there began the switch from a hunting-and-gathering way of life. They learned how to grow grains, vegetables, and fruit; how to domesticate cattle, sheep, hogs, horses, goats, and oxen. They settled in villages not

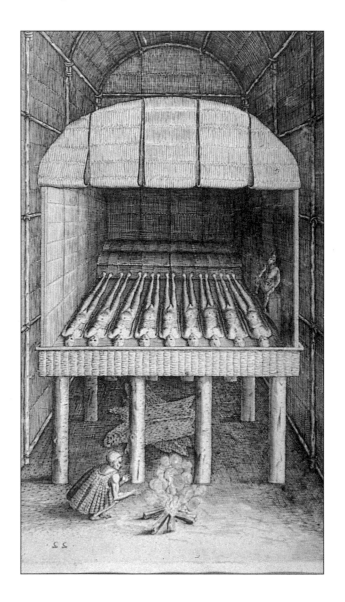

According to de Bry, this was an Indian charnel house, or place where the dead were prepared for burial. From the 1590 Hariot report.

(left) De Bry entitled this picture "Their Manner of Carrying Children and the Attire of the Chief Ladies of the Town of Dasemonquepeuc."

(below) "A Chief Lady of Pomeiooc" was the caption given to this engraving by deBry.

much different from the Algonquian ones. The villages grew into towns. Slowly at first, but with gathering momentum, the Europeans increased their technical skills. They learned to smelt metal from ores and turn the metal into axes, swords, plow blades, and armor. They made equally momentous inventions like the alphabet and writing, the concept of zero, and the decimal system of counting. They learned something about how the human body, and animal life in general, works. Many of these inventions and discoveries were made not in Europe proper, but around the eastern end of the Mediterranean in the civilizations of Egypt, Mesopotamia, Assyria, and Babylonia. Europeans were quick to take over the most important of these ideas and proceeded to develop them. By twenty-five hundred years ago there existed in Greece a high civilization in which art, literature, philosophy, and the beginnings of science flourished.

Over the next centuries a culture spread across Europe that grew out of Greece and Rome, to which religious elements from the Near East—especially Christianity—were added. By the 1400s a unified culture existed in Europe, which was remarkably similar from Sicily to Scandinavia. There were variations, of course. The warmer climate south of the Alps made for differences in agriculture, dress, and ways of life, from those of the colder north. Nonetheless, there was a striking unity to European culture. People grew the same sorts of crops and kept the same domestic animals across the breadth of the continent. Metal was worked in the same way to make the same kinds of tools. Dwellings were made of brick or mud and wattles and thatched. A great religious architecture produced similar types of cathedrals everywhere. Autocratic monarchs, supported by wealthy aristocracies of dukes and earls, ruled small duchies, principalities, and city-states. But by the fifteenth century the new scheme of the large nation-state was coming into being. Germany and Italy were still conglomerations of princedoms and city-states, but France, England, and Spain were emerging as unified nations with established borders and common languages.

Another de Bry picture shows an Indian method of broiling meat, which includes alligator, fish, and two animals hard to identify.

One religion, Roman Catholicism, using virtually the same form of worship in similar churches, covered the whole European continent, although by the 1500s splinter movements were growing. Ordinary people did not read, but the tiny minority of educated people all spoke and read one language—Latin—as well as their native tongues. There were no passports in the modern sense, and the educated, the wealthy, artists, and musicians frequently traveled with ease from one country to the next.

There were substantial differences between European and Indian cultures. For one, the Europeans were technologically well ahead of the Indians. But as we shall see, differences in *attitudes* were perhaps more critical. And, as much of the clash of these two cultures involved the use

Indians harvesting wild rice. Rice eventually became an important crop for the European settlers who came into the Carolinas.

of land, it is especially important to see how the two groups thought about ownership.

As we have seen, the Indians had no great interest in piling up wealth. This was particularly true of land. A village, or several villages, might have the use of a stretch of woods, a river, or a lake for certain purposes, but there was no exclusive right of ownership by which land could be bought or sold, any more than we today can conceive of owning and selling the air around us.

The Europeans had a different idea. They believed very strongly in the private ownership of property: What's mine is mine and I can do what I want with it. My land could be passed down to my heirs forever. Land, thus, was not an inseparable part of the environment as it was for the Indians, but a commodity to be bought and sold just like any transportable object. This concept probably grew out of the fact that huge portions of Europe had been converted to farmland; there were few open forests to share for hunting and gathering. Ownership of land was the key

This painting is thought to be a good illustration of a typical English village of the time when the English were bringing their culture to America.

not only to wealth, but to prestige: The more land you owned, the more important and powerful you were. Indians, on the other hand, gained individual power and importance by being valorous in battle, skilled at hunting, and having leadership qualities like eloquence and wit.

The Indians were not exclusivist like the Europeans. Indians saw no reason why you couldn't worship both their gods and those of the Englishman at the same time. They expected the new arrivals to join their villages and families and marry their daughters. But for European Christians there was only one god and the worship of any other was a mortal sin. And though many settlers ran away to live with Indians, even fully adopting their lifestyles, English officials and social mores were strongly opposed to such integration, and those who were caught attempting it were severely punished—even by death.

The two peoples, thus, had very different ways of viewing the world and acting in it. Though for the first few months of contact in various places each group thought and hoped for friendly relations, it seems clear to us today, looking back, that the cultures were destined to clash.

CHAPTER III

Indians Repulse the European Invaders

In Europe wealth and power came mainly through land. But there was one other way of getting wealth, which by the 1400s was becoming increasingly important, and that was trade. The great trick in trade was to find some sort of goods that were unavailable in your own land, but plentiful some place else; for then you could buy them cheap, bring them home, and sell them for good prices. With the profits, you could buy yet larger amounts of such goods and quickly multiply your wealth.

Europeans had been trading among themselves for a long time. Wheat from the Baltic area was sold to the Mediterranean countries; wool from England went to Antwerp and Amsterdam. But the big money was to be made by importing luxury goods from the Indies. Spices from Indonesia, silks from Japan, and textiles from India trickled in by caravan across an overland route through Persia (now Iran) and Turkey. But these caravan trips were expensive, time-consuming, and dangerous, for bandits could, and did, swoop down on caravans and make off with the precious goods. By 1400 Europeans were looking for a safer sea route to the East. The Portuguese, inspired by their Prince Henry, called the Navigator, began to explore south along the African coast. By the late 1400s they had turned the corner around the bottom of Africa, and eventually they pushed on to India and then China.

But others were looking in another direction. It is usually believed that Christopher Columbus set out from Spain in order to prove that the world was round. In fact, some two thousand years earlier, Greek philosophers had concluded that the world was a sphere and even calculated that it was 21,420 miles in circumference, not far from the correct 24,875. Among educated people, at least, the idea that the world was a globe was widely accepted.

It was obvious, then, that a ship could reach the riches of the East by sailing west. Even so, it was believed that the trip was too long to be practical. Columbus, however, had made his own calculations and decided that the distance was much less than others believed. He developed an almost religious conviction that he had a mission to find the western route to the Indies, which might also lead to Christianizing the inhabitants and saving them from an eternal afterlife in hell. For a long time he tried to persuade powerful and wealthy people to finance the trip, but they all believed it was foolhardy. Finally, early in 1492, Columbus persuaded the Spanish sovereigns, Ferdinand and Isabella, to pay for the wild trip west. He struck a hard bargain, demanding the title of Admiral of the Ocean Sea and control of whatever lands he found.

On August 3 he sailed aboard the *Santa Maria*, accompanied by two smaller ships, the *Niña* and the *Pinta*. For a month the travelers were out of sight of land. The sailors grew frightened and demanded that Columbus turn back. He made a persuasive speech, and they agreed to continue. Finally, on October 12, at two in the morning, a lookout on the *Pinta* saw moonlight shining on a limestone cliff. It must have been an incredible moment: We can imagine the excitement of all on board as they strained through the dark to see what sort of land they had come to. At dawn Columbus anchored off an island in the Bahamas. (We are not exactly sure which one it was.)

Christopher Columbus. This picture was restored from an earlier one, and the clothing is probably not accurate.

Unfortunately, the new land was a disappointment. Columbus found the gentle Arawak Indians, but no gold. He then sailed to Cuba, where again he found no gold, but he did find something that would prove very important to American history—a plant the Indians "drank" the smoke of, called tobacco. Neither on this trip nor on subsequent ones did Columbus find the fabulous riches of the Indies he had gone out after, and he died in poverty. To top it off, the credit for having discovered the New World went to another man. A Florentine named Amerigo Vespucci made several trips to South America in the years around 1500. He was not an

Amerigo Vespucci, using a navigational instrument called the astrolabe. He was not an important explorer, but by chance he had the western hemisphere named for him.

important explorer, but in 1504–1505 letters were published crediting him with the discovery of the New World, and very quickly the name America was fastened onto the whole vast Western Hemisphere. Not until long after he was dead did Christopher Columbus get the credit.

Actually, it is clear enough that Columbus did not "discover" America, either. The Indians, of course, had discovered it at least twenty thousand years before. Other Europeans had got there earlier, too. Perhaps some Irish who had gone across the chain of islands at the north end of the Atlantic to Iceland had visited in the 800s; the Norse sailor Erik the Red colonized Greenland in about 985, and there were little Norse towns there for several centuries; his son, Leif the Lucky, landed on the North American coast and established summer encampments in Newfoundland in about 1000. But these early ventures to the New World were soon forgotten.

Others who may have seen the New World before Columbus were fishermen sailing out of Bristol, England. Europeans ate millions of pounds of cheap, nutritious fish every week. The North Atlantic, especially in the area off Canada and Maine, was filled with fish—cod, in particular—which proved to be easy to cure and store. Bristol fishermen may have been working this area by the 1480s and may even have landed on the American coast, but kept it quiet so as to keep this information of this prime fishing ground to themselves. But eventually Portuguese and French fishermen joined the English in the North Atlantic fishing grounds.

One Bristol man who definitely reached North America quite early was a transplanted Venetian, John Cabot. He persuaded King Henry VII to support a trip to find a route to the Indies and in 1497 landed on the American coast, possibly in Newfoundland. However, he brought back no silks, spices, and gold. He later made a second trip, from which he never returned.

To the south events were moving at a more rapid pace. The development of Spanish America from Mexico down to the bottom of the hemisphere is not really part of our story. Nonetheless, we should know that very soon after the well-publicized voyages of Columbus, other daring and ambitious men began to colonize the Caribbean Islands. They went on to conquer the large, advanced civilizations of the Inca of Peru and the Aztec and Maya of southern Mexico. These conquests were utterly amazing: Within a few short years a handful of Spanish *conquistadores* subdued whole empires of tens of thousands of people. They were aided by the possession of horses, firearms, and armor, but they would not have succeeded had not the Indians been enmeshed in struggles between warring factions and had not the Indians been destroyed by the spread of lethal European diseases. By the mid-1500s the Spanish were in command of huge chunks of the land south of the Rio Grande and were sending home incredible tons of jewelry, and gold and silver mined by Indian slaves.

Between the conquests of the Spanish in the south and the tentative explorations of other Europeans in the north, by the early 1500s it was clear that the lands across the Atlantic were not the Indies, but a new and strange country, previously unknown to Europeans. Interest was immense, especially when the astonishing wealth being taken home by the Spanish became known. Other ambitious men raised money one way or another and set out on voyages of discovery. Some of them were looking for gold and silver; others saw money to be made from more practical goods like fish and timber; yet others were looking for the elusive passage through the continent to the Indies. The Spanish made some explorations in North America, especially along the Gulf of Mexico, up the Mississippi, and into Florida. In 1524 an Italian, Giovanni da Verrazano, sailed up the North American coast as far as Casco Bay, where Portland, Maine, is today. In 1534 a Frenchman, Jacques Cartier, explored the region around the Saint Lawrence River. The map of the North American shoreline began to fill in.

The great French explorer Jacques Cartier. He failed in his search for the elusive Northwest Passage, but in the course of it discovered the St. Lawrence region, which he claimed for France, thus laying the basis for the development of the French colony in what is now Canada.

Most significantly, explorers like Verrazano and Cartier began to make contact with the native peoples, the Indians. In part the Europeans were simply curious, and on a few occasions they kidnapped Indians and carried them back to Europe as curiosities, as slaves, or so that the Indians could learn European languages and act as translators. But we must keep in mind that the original impulse for the western explorations had been to make money through trade in the Indies. Making money was

The English liked to portray the Spanish conquerors of Central and South America as particularly cruel, and they encouraged the Indians to rise up against their masters. This de Bry engraving shows Indians bearing heavy burdens under the swords of the Spanish.

still uppermost in the minds of the Europeans. One item they quickly discovered could be profitable was beaver skins. At the time, and for two centuries afterwards, there was a fashion in Europe for wide-brimmed, high-crowned hats made of felt. Beaver fur made excellent felt.

The fishermen and explorers began trading for beaver pelts. The Indians were especially attracted to European metal goods, like copper and iron cooking pots, knives, and hatchets, as well as beads, pins, and

Another depiction of Spanish cruelty, by de Bry. Here Indian slaves are forced to work in salt mines by their Spanish masters.

necklaces of metal. By the mid-1500s trade between Europeans and certain groups of Indians with access to beaver pelts, especially in Maine and further north, was well established.

This sounds innocuous enough, but in fact the beaver trade foreshadowed the destruction of the Indian way of life that was to come. Through the 1500s the Indians' appetite for European metal goods grew, especially for weapons that would give them substantial advantage over enemies in war. From hunting beaver in their usual conservative and saving way, they went to ripping apart beaver houses and dams and indiscriminately slaughtering whole populations of beaver, males, females, and infants. Beaver were no longer part of the bounty of nature, a helpful part of the environment; they were now a commodity to be bought and sold. The time taken for beaver hunting cut into the time needed for getting food, and the time Indian women put into preparing the beaver skins prevented them from tending their gardens. The beaver-hunting Indians then had to trade European goods for corn with Indians farther south. The beaver, inevitably, began to grow scarce. The balanced relationship most Indians had developed with nature in the beaver country was broken. For the beaver Indians there was no thought of fighting off the encroaching Europeans; they needed them. For the Indians, the new form of beaver trade was an evil omen. They had taken into their culture a pattern, philosophy, and way of life that was foreign to it. And as with a human swallowing a foreign substance, their old culture was poisoned. The clash of cultures was no less deadly for being subtle and silent.

The Indians did not see the danger, because at first the Europeans appeared not to pose much of a threat. There were too few of them, and their visits were irregular. So long as the whites kept their distance, the Indians believed they had little to fear from these strange-looking people with their odd ways.

And at first the Europeans did not encroach on Indian territory. They were mainly fishing offshore or looking for a passage through the land.

But inevitably, in time the Europeans began to think of establishing themselves on the shore. They wanted trading posts. The Spanish wanted small forts in Florida to protect their treasure fleets from marauders. More generally, the rivalrous European nations were afraid that somebody else would move in and take over this land with its enormous potential. The Spanish were already making themselves into the mightiest nation in Europe on the strength of Latin American treasures, or so it seemed. What would happen if they—or anybody—took over North America as well?

However, the Indians were frequently able to fight back. This de Bry engraving shows Indians massacring Spanish at Cumaná, in what is now Venezuela.

And so, throughout the second half of the 1500s, European governments and merchants tried to settle the new land with Europeans. Again and again they crossed the ocean with shiploads of soldiers, adventurers, prisoners, and even the poor dragged off the streets; again and again they built palisaded settlements armed with cannons; again and again the settlements failed. Part of the problem was the European rivalries themselves: For example, in 1565 a French settlement in Florida was attacked by the Spanish. The settlers, already starving, surrendered, and the Spanish slaughtered them to a man.

A second difficulty was the Europeans' misunderstanding about the American climate. They believed that all around the world places at the same latitude would have similar climates. New England was at the same latitude as Spain, and it was assumed the area was a subtropical paradise where food fell from the trees. A colony founded at Sagadahoc, in Maine, collapsed when the colonists were subjected to a New England winter for which they were unprepared.

But the main reason why the Europeans had so much difficulty establishing themselves in the New World was simple: The Indians did not want them there. By the mid-1500s the Indians had had enough experience with the Europeans to realize that they were not always friendly. By the time that Verrazano sailed into Casco Bay in 1524 he found the Indians there cautious indeed:

> If we wanted to trade with them for some of their things, they would come to the seashore on some rocks where the breakers were most violent, while we remained on the little boat, and they sent us what they wanted to give on rope, continually shouting for us not to approach the land; they gave us the barter quickly, and would take in exchange only knives, hooks for fishing, and sharp metal [i.e. knives and axes]. We found no courtesy in them, and when we had

nothing more to exchange and left them, they made all the signs of scorn and shame that any brute creatures would make.

Yet Verrazano, on the same voyage, found himself cordially welcomed by the Narragansett in Rhode Island who, he said, were "the most beautiful and have the most civil customs we have found on this voyage."

The Indians' feelings toward the Europeans were mixed, depending on the experience that they had had with them. On the one hand, they were impressed by English technology—the large ships that could cross the great sea, the metal tools like axes and fishhooks, woven cloth, and especially their weapons. Guns in particular seemed to the Indians almost magical, producing noise, fire, smoke, and instant death with no apparent cause. On the other hand, the Indians were somewhat scornful of the whites: They constantly floundered in the woods, which were like playgrounds to the Indians; they did not seem to be able to get food for themselves; and they lacked the iron will of Indian males in the face of hardship. In sum, the Indians were wary of the whites, but by no means overawed by them.

In any case, through the 1500s, they were able to fend the Europeans off—in part, due to errors and misjudgments made by the intruders. Through the second half of the 1500s' the Indians easily halted at least half a dozen attempts by French and Spanish invaders to establish settlements on the Atlantic coast of what we now call Florida and North and South Carolina.

But pressure for colonization, especially in England, was growing. The clash of cultures was now about to be joined in earnest.

CHAPTER IV

The Cultures Clash on the Chesapeake

After the death of Henry VIII in 1547, England was torn by deadly religious battling, in which each side shed the blood of its opponents as they came to power in turn. (For more detail on the religious upheavals in England at this time see *Pilgrims and Puritans*, book three in this series.) However, in 1558 Elizabeth I began a reign that would last for almost fifty years. She was a subtle and clever compromiser, and very quickly she subdued the quarreling factions. An era of prosperity began, accompanied by a glorious period in the arts and sciences, which included the plays of William Shakespeare. English pride grew; English people, from the great lords in their manors to farmers in their thatched huts, felt that England was destined to become the greatest of nations.

It seemed particularly important to the English not to let the wealthy and powerful Spanish, who in 1588 attempted to invade England, dominate the New World. Furthermore, it was clear that a lot of money could be made out of America, although nobody was exactly sure how. England was also suffering from a surplus of workers. The population had been growing all through the 1500s, and on top of it, big landowners were

Elizabeth I was the first English monarch to take a serious interest in America. She sponsored Sir Walter Raleigh's first trips, leading the way to the settlement of Virginia. The region was named for her, although she was dead by the time the first permanent colony was founded there.

This early map of portions of the eastern seaboard of North America shows Virginia, where the English were about to establish themselves, and Florida, which was claimed by the Spanish. The Europeans' ability to make good maps was critical to their success in exploring and colonizing the New World. This map was published by the famous mapmaker Gerhard Mercator in Amsterdam in 1606, the year before Jamestown was founded.

fencing off their estates in order to raise sheep and cattle, a process that was throwing tens of thousands of tenant farmers off the land. These people were wandering city streets and country highways, looking for work, and begging and stealing when they couldn't find jobs. Why not settle them in the empty spaces of America? And beyond all of this, the English, like most Europeans, honestly believed they had a duty to Christianize "heathens" elsewhere, in order to save them from eternal damnation in hell.

The English, then, had lots of reasons for colonizing North America. They were, however, slow to get going. Elizabeth had in her court a bold, charming, and intelligent young man named Walter Raleigh, who was rapidly becoming her favorite. With Elizabeth's backing, in 1583 Raleigh made the first of several futile attempts to establish a settlement in the Chesapeake Bay area, part of a stretch of land from the Hudson River to the Carolinas that the English called Virginia, after the virgin queen. It today seems presumptuous for somebody to simply hand over to a European monarch a huge chunk of land already occupied by other people. But the English felt that the "savages," as they saw them, would quickly see the advantages of English ways, particularly Christianity, and would adopt English

Sir Walter Raleigh, a brave and charming courtier and a favorite of Elizabeth I, persuaded her to permit the development of the Virginia colony. Although Raleigh himself was not successful in establishing an American outpost, his efforts opened the doors for later English colonization.

customs. Life would be better for them. Whatever the rights and wrongs, over the next several years Raleigh tried to establish a settlement in the Chesapeake region. Each effort failed due to disease, starvation, mischance, and the hostility of the Indians, who were no more willing to give up their religion and other core elements of their culture than the English were. The English gave up trying and so did the Indians.

But the reasons for American settlement remained strong, and in 1607 another group, under Elizabeth's successor, James I, tried again. In the spring of 1607 the colonizers set off, and on May 14 they landed at what they called Jamestown Island. (The settlement of Jamestown is described in *The Paradox of Jamestown*, book two of this series.) They were carrying with them a secret weapon, the importance of which neither they nor the Indians yet knew, although it had already been at work. That was disease.

The American Indians were a remarkably healthy people. They were taller than the Europeans and had better teeth and fewer illnesses. Part of their good health was due to a superior diet: While most Indians suffered from "hunger times," on the whole they ate a full and varied diet gathered from a land rich in animal and plant life.

Another reason for the Indians' better health was the absence among them of an array of viruses and bacteria that were present everywhere in Europe. In the Old World, diseases like smallpox, bubonic plague, influenza, and measles were scourges, killing millions every year. These diseases were a constant menace, sometimes dying down and then flaring up again. The so-called Black Death of the 1300s killed half the people in Paris, three-quarters in Florence. In 1625, forty-one thousand people died of the plague in London alone. Contrary to what is often said, the Europeans were not immune to such diseases.

But they did have *relative* immunity. For biological reasons, a group of people subject to a disease will gradually acquire some resistance to it. By the time of the early English explorations of America, Europeans assumed that a large percentage of them would catch smallpox but only a quarter or fewer would die from it.

Tragically, the Indians had virtually no immunity to these European diseases. The diseases did not exist in the New World, for reasons not fully understood. But by the 1500s the Indians were at deadly risk from plague, smallpox, and influenza. The European soldiers, sailors, fishermen, and traders who were landing in the New World in the 1500s often carried deadly bacteria and viruses on their clothing, their blankets, or themselves. As they moved around the Americas they left behind a series of devastating epidemics.

One of the worst was among the earliest, an epidemic of smallpox that raged between 1520 and 1524. Through the 1500s there were other smallpox epidemics in New England, the Great Lakes region, and Mexico, and similar epidemics of measles, deadly to the unprotected Indians, in 1531–33, 1592–93, and 1602. There were also epidemics of influenza, typhus, diphtheria, and the plague.

These epidemics were earth-scorching. They usually—not just occasionally—killed 90 or even 95 percent of the affected people. Whole clusters of villages were wiped out, depopulating large areas. Years later there would be found in weedy cornfields the scattered bones of scores of people who died there, leaving behind no one to bury them.

Unfortunately, the Indians did not understand that such diseases were passed from person to person, and they made matters worse by sitting with ill relatives to comfort them. Both they and the Europeans believed that these afflictions had been brought on them by the Christian god. To the Indians this was a sign that the white man's god was stronger than theirs. The Europeans, too, believed this and took it as a sign that God was clearing the way for them to take over the new land.

We can see how complex this clash of European and Indian culture could be. It was not just ways of thinking or differences in technology that mattered. The very types of diseases that each people harbored was critical. There is no question in the minds of historians that the European diseases were a crucial factor—perhaps *the* crucial factor—in the struggle between these two peoples for the land. This was a weapon the Indians could not fight.

Initially, the Jamestown settlers were mainly soldiers and were coming, in a sense, as invaders. They were up against a people well able to defend their land. These people were a collection of tribes of Algonquian who had come under the command of a cunning and aggressive leader known as Powhatan. Many years before, Powhatan had inherited leadership of a group of tribes. For three decades he had been bringing additional tribes under his control through war, alliance, and gift giving. His control was firm, but not absolute; some tribes were only loosely ruled by Powhatan, others were more tightly held. Powhatan ruled over an area around the York and James Rivers, containing about twelve thousand people. He was no less arrogant than the English and considered himself the equal, if not the superior, of King James. He had no intention of letting the English walk over him.

The English settlers chose to establish themselves up the James River on a peninsula, where they would have ample notice of a Spanish attack. The water here was deep enough to take large ships. It was swampy and bred diseases that killed many of the colonists, but the swamps and the river protected the site from both Indian and Spanish attack.

Hostilities began immediately, when the Indians attacked a party of scouts sent out from the ship, wounding two men. The English set about building a wooden fort. Twelve days later some of the English leaders went upriver to be entertained by a local Indian chief. While they were gone another group of several hundred Indians attacked the fort, killing two Englishmen and wounding a dozen more. The English, aided by the ships' cannons, drove them off.

What the English did not know was that both the Indians who were entertaining the English leaders and the ones who attacked the fort were

A sixteenth-century European engraver's imaginative portrayal of the great chief Powhatan at a council. The general idea is correct. Indian dwellings were made of mats tied over frames, and Powhatan did like to meet people with his many wives gathered around him.

under Powhatan's command. This is an extremely significant point. The astute Powhatan assumed that he could drive the English out of his territory any time he decided to. The interlopers had firearms, that was true. But Powhatan had them so badly outnumbered he was sure he could triumph relatively easily.

But did he want to drive them out? As we have seen, much of Indian politics involved the making and breaking of alliances for tribute, protection, or to war against mutual enemies. Powhatan had built a small empire through such maneuvers. As was frequently the case with Indians, Powhatan was at odds with several tribes on his borders, such as the Iroquois-speaking Susquehannocks to the north. His first thought was to make the English a useful ally against his various enemies. English guns, he was sure, would give him an overpowering advantage.

His tactic, it appears, was first to impress the English with the idea that they needed an Indian ally through an attack, and then to offer his friendship. He began trading corn to the English, who were without provisions, in exchange for metal hatchets and knives he could use against his enemies. Despite his help, during that first summer nearly half the English colony died from hunger and disease. The English lacked good leadership, had trouble coping with wilderness conditions, and were in general disorganized. Among other things, they were not much interested in hard work and failed to plant enough corn to see them through. Luckily, there was among them an intelligent, resourceful, and ambitious man, who quickly rose to leadership through his abilities. His name was John Smith, and he has become an American legend, featured in movies, for a lot of wrong reasons.

Unlike many of the colonial leaders, Smith was not an aristocrat but from a yeoman family. He had some schooling and then went off to fight in European wars, which was one way for an ambitious young man to make a mark. He fought against the Turks and was captured and made a slave in Constantinople. He escaped with the help of a "beautiful princess" and visited Russia and then North America before getting back to England. When he came to Virginia at age twenty-four he was a man of considerable experience with both warfare and strange cultures. Smith began getting the colonists organized.

Then, only a few months after the founding of the Jamestown settlement, Smith was captured by a large party of Powhatan's Indians under the leadership of Powhatan's brother Opechancanough. He spent a month with the Indians and learned a lot about them, which would come in handy later. Eventually he was taken to see the great Powhatan himself. Smith was talking to Powhatan, showing him proper deference, and explaining that the English did not intend to stay in Virginia but would leave, which was not true. Suddenly, the conversation was broken off, and Smith was assaulted by a number of warriors who intended "to beate out his braines." At that moment Powhatan's daughter jumped in between Smith and the Indians, "got his head in her armes, and laid her owne upon his to save him from death."

The Indian woman was, of course, Pocahontas. The whole story has been the subject of much mythmaking and is probably untrue. Historians today believe that Smith misunderstood what was happening, and that the "attack" by the warriors was part of some kind of ceremony, perhaps adopting John Smith into the tribe. It is probable that Powhatan wanted to keep Smith alive, so he could work through him to use the English for his own purposes.

For a time peaceful relations prevailed. But Powhatan kept raising the price for his corn and in the end began demanding muskets in trade. The English refused, because, quite sensibly, they did not wish to arm the Indians. Relationships deteriorated, corn grew short among the English, and finally Smith decided on a get-tough policy. At first he was able to intimidate the Indians into giving him the corn he needed to feed the colony, but eventually they refused. Smith then began raiding Indian villages. The conflict broke into open warfare.

Attacks by the English were answered by vengeance, as was the Indian custom, and by the winter of 1609 the vastly larger forces of Powhatan had the English pinned into their fort. Food grew short and then disappeared, and the English began what came to be known as the starving time. They ate their hogs, their hens, their goats, and their horses; then they began to eat dogs, cats, rats, and mice. Some boiled their boots and ate them. One man actually killed his wife and ate her. Others went out into the woods looking for anything they could find and were killed by Indians. Their bodies were eaten by the settlers still alive. Finally, when one of the officers of the Virginia Company arrived from Bermuda, he was so shocked by the condition of the settlers that he ordered Jamestown abandoned. Powhatan had won, or so it seemed. The English were actually aboard ship when three English vessels filled with supplies, one hundred fifty new colonists, and one hundred soldiers came sailing into the James River.

Now war began in earnest. The English no longer believed they could convert the Indians to Christianity or "civilize" them, and they were determined to drive them away. All male adults in the settlement were in effect soldiers and were required to practice with muskets. The English began raiding Indian villages for corn, sometimes murdering Indians and burning villages. Powhatan fought back, killing the English when he caught them outside the fort. In 1611 the Indians besieged Jamestown again, and they might have driven the English away, but a fleet of ships with reinforcements and supplies again arrived to raise the siege.

The English were now equipped with heavy armor, which was impervious to arrows, and the new "snaphaunce" muskets, which could be fired faster than their older guns. Their corn raids became so effective that Indian warriors had to spend much time clearing new, hidden fields for planting.

Then in 1613 the English captured Pocahontas. They demanded a huge ransom in corn for her return, and some muskets that Powhatan had got hold of. Powhatan refused. In the spring of 1614 the English and the Indian leaders met. There were threats and counterthreats, but in the end Powhatan, by now an old man, gave in, agreeing to make peace. The English were established as a power in what had once been Powhatan's lands. Shortly thereafter Pocahontas converted to Christianity and married a leading colonist, John Rolfe. Not only had Powhatan surrendered a portion of his power, but his daughter had married into the enemy camp.

Two of the most famous people in early American history, John Smith and Pocahontas. Smith was a resourceful man who almost singlehandedly saved the Jamestown Colony during an early crisis. Pocahontas converted to English ways and took the name Rebecca. In 1616 she visited England with her husband, John Rolfe, and some other Indians. This picture was made at that time. The famous story of her saving Smith's life is probably mostly legend.

But Rolfe would play a far more important role in the history of the United States. Pipe smoking was now widely popular throughout Europe, and the Spanish were making fortunes from tobacco grown in their Caribbean island colonies. Rolfe began experiments in an effort to improve the local tobacco grown in Virginia by the Indians. It was of inferior quality, but he managed to get hold of some seeds of the Caribbean variety. It proved to be satisfactory, and by 1618 he was shipping tobacco to England, where it commanded excellent prices. Quickly other colonists began planting tobacco, and suddenly Virginia became tobacco mad, to the point where colonial leaders had to pass laws requiring landowners

The cultivation of tobacco for the European market was what allowed the English colony first to survive and then to grow prosperous. This early drawing of the tobacco plant appeared in a book in 1570, long before Jamestown was founded, suggesting the great interest in smoking in Europe.

This old wood-cut shows a seventeenth-century tobacco shop where people gathered to smoke. The wooden statue of an Indian to the left was a sign for the shop. Note the pipes in the wheel at top left.

to plant corn so the colony wouldn't starve. Tobacco, in the end, would make Virginia self-sufficient.

For a few years after the treaty with Powhatan there was relative peace, broken only by an occasional skirmish. Then, beginning in 1617, the Virginia Indians were hit by another series of the epidemics the

Europeans had brought. The elderly Powhatan died in 1618 and was replaced by his brother Opechancanough. The new chief had a long list of grievances against the English and had been biding his time. A series of incidents, in which both English and Indians were killed, raised tensions. In 1622 Opechancanough decided to strike hard and rid himself of the English once and for all.

On the morning of March 22, 1622, hundreds of Opechancanough's warriors poured out of the woods and attacked farms and settlements along the James and Appomattox Rivers. The Indians wiped out 347 men, women, and children, about a third of the entire Virginia colony. If Opechancanough had rapidly followed up his initial strike with an attack on Jamestown itself, he could easily have finished off the colony, discouraging further attempts by Europeans to settle the land and changing the history of America.

But once again cultural differences had their effect. An Indian tribe that had suffered so grievous a wound would have concluded that it was overmatched and would have withdrawn. But contrary to Opechancanough's expectations, the English resolve stiffened. For the rest of the year the colonists went out again and again on forays, killing Indians, taking corn, and sometimes burning villages. Finally, in July 1624, sixty well-armored Englishmen sailed up the York into the heart of Opechancanough's territory. They were vastly outnumbered by some eight hundred Indian warriors, who decided to make a fight of it. For two days they battled in the open, something that the Indians rarely did. The Indians showed great courage and determination, so that even the English expressed admiration of them, but courage and determination were not enough against steel armor and snaphaunce muskets. The Indians suffered many casualties; the English had only sixteen wounded and none dead.

In the end the Indians had no choice but to withdraw. Indians from some other tribes observed the battle, and the inability of a brave force of

Indians to defeat a tiny English army impressed them. At that point the war between what once had been Powhatan's mighty confederation and the English was effectively over. There would be, for many years, occasional skirmishes, with killing on both sides. But there was no longer any possibility of the Indians running the English out of the Virginia area. The English had won the clash of cultures in Virginia.

CHAPTER V

The Cultures Clash
in New England

Meanwhile, six hundred miles to the north, a similar cultural clash was working itself out. The story of the Pilgrims, the Puritans, Plymouth Rock, and the Massachusetts Bay Colony is well known. To simplify, the 1500s in England and in other places in Europe were a time of religious upheaval. Several different groups were competing with the dominant church—the official Anglican Church—to establish their own type of worship. One major strain was a "purifying" movement, which wanted to cut down on the pomp and ceremony left over from Roman Catholic practices. Some of these English Puritans wanted to carry it further and separate themselves from the national church. Eventually a small group of these "Separatists" moved to Holland, where there was greater religious tolerance.

However, after a few years, Separatist elders concluded that life among the easygoing Dutch was drawing many of the group, especially the young, away from their religious calling. They decided, then, to see if they could build a new Jerusalem in the wilderness of North America.

Once again, the English gave little thought to the people who occupied the land. Like the Jamestown colonists, they assumed that the rude savages, as they saw them, who peopled North America would be impressed by English life, European technology, and Christianity. They would soon adopt English ways, and the two peoples would live in harmony, sharing the land.

These people were coming to America with goals different from those of the Virginia colonists. The Jamestown people were basically after profit. The Pilgrims wanted to build a religious community—what they called a City of God. They were not simply members of the same church; they were a tight-knit community of people who saw themselves as special, favored by God. To them life and religion were one and the same. Whatever we may feel about this sense of religious mission among the Pilgrims, it is hardly uncommon even today, when bloody battling between religious groups regularly makes headlines. But it was bound to cause trouble between the Indians and the whites. (Readers who would like more detail on the founding of the Massachusetts colonies will find it in *Pilgrims and Puritans*, the third book of this series.)

Meanwhile, fate was preparing the ground for the English. In 1617 the plague that had killed Powhatan reached New England. It struck particularly hard in the most populous areas, as epidemics usually do. One of these was the area of the coast from Massachusetts Bay where Boston now stands, south to Plymouth, and then out to Cape Cod.

This stretch of land had been affluent. Much of it had been cleared of forest and turned into fields for corn, beans, and squash. The Indians also had an abundance of shellfish from the shores, cod from the sea, salmon from the rivers, deer and other game from the woods. They had built villages up and down the coast and developed a pleasant way of living there, although it included much of the warfare that was traditional among the Algonquian.

The epidemic destroyed much of this life. Some villages lost 95 percent of their inhabitants, leaving the few survivors to creep away to the shelter of other villages. The fields filled up with weeds and brush, which often grew up around the bones of dozens of bodies left unburied. Indian groups to the north and west, which had escaped the plague, came down on the now weakened coastal tribes.

This was the situation the Pilgrims aboard the *Mayflower* came into in 1620. They found a land of empty villages, and fields ready for planting. Unfortunately, it was November when they landed, and nothing could be planted. They suffered dreadfully that first year, during which time half of the colonists died from disease and malnutrition. They found some baskets of dried corn buried in Indian graves, which helped. More important was the aid of the famous Squanto. He had been captured by earlier English explorers and had spent some time in England, where he learned English. He eventually escaped and made his way back to New England shortly before the Pilgrims landed. He discovered his entire village empty, his people dead from the plague. He was glad to see the Pilgrims when they landed, for he needed them as much as they needed him. He showed them how to plant corn in the spring. The harvest feast they held in the fall of 1621 was, of course, our first Thanksgiving.

Bit by bit the Plymouth Colony struggled to its feet. Initially, the Indians were suspicious of the English. Their attitude was much the same as Powhatan's had been. They admired English technology—the metal tools, the guns, the great sailing vessels. But they had no intention of letting the English simply take over. In fact, the Wampanoag tribe, which had been hard hit by the epidemic, were more fearful of the Narragansett tribe to the south than they were of the small English colony. And as had been the case with the Virginia Indians, they began jockeying to see if they could get the English to help them against their Indian enemies.

For example, in 1621, when the little Plymouth Colony was desperately trying to hang on, Massasoit, a chief of the Pokanoket, a tribe residing between the Massachusett and Narragansett, approached Governor William Bradford with an offer of alliance. Each would aid the other in case it was attacked. Only afterward did the English discover that

Massasoit was already at war with the Narragansett and was hoping to bring English muskets in on his side. Another Massachusett chief, Chicatabot, was also bickering with the Narragansett. He told the English that the Narragansett were about to attack them. He then arranged for some Narragansett warriors to see the English making

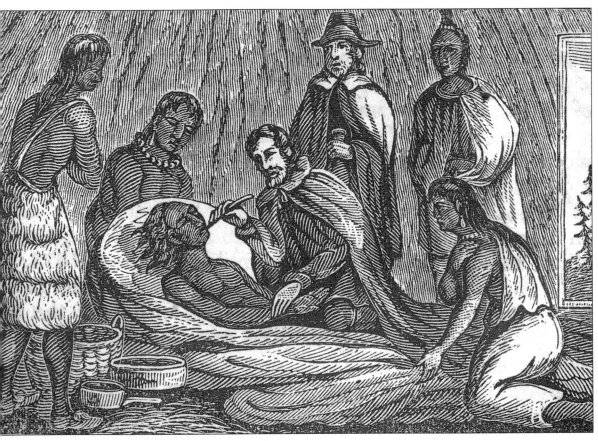

Despite everything, the New England colonists managed to remain on good terms with the Pokanoket, led by the famous chief Massasoit, with whom the English signed a peace treaty not long after their arrival. This early woodcut is entitled "Mr. Winslow, attending on Massasoit." Winslow was one of the Pilgrim leaders.

preparation to do battle with them, and by threatening them with the English attack, Chicatabot made the Narragansett back down.

Nor was Squanto aiding the English colony solely out of the goodness of his heart. He threatened to bring his English friends down on his Indian enemies if they did not pay him tribute. When this did not work, he tried to get the English to attack his enemies by telling them that some Indians, including Massasoit, were combining to attack the Plymouth Colony. This trick, too, failed, and Squanto was forced to hide out among the English for the remaining year of his life.

This kind of diplomatic maneuvering had long been customary among the Indians. Shifting alliances were usual. To a considerable extent, instead of seeing the English as their common enemy, the Indians used them as just one more player in the game.

Over several years, tension between the Indians and the English increased. Part of the problem lay in the cultural differences: Neither side quite understood why the others did some of the things they did. For example, once friendship between the two peoples was established, the Indians felt free to come and go in the English settlement as they liked. However, the English, who valued their solidarity as a religious community, disliked this stream of casual visits, which often involved feeding their visitors, and forbade the Indians to come uninvited. On the other side, some English once spent a night in what they took to be an empty Indian hut. It had been abandoned because its owner had recently died, as was the Indians' rule, and the English intrusion was considered sacrilegious. Misunderstandings of these kinds constantly raised hackles on both sides.

A second problem was that Myles Standish, one of the Pilgrim leaders, was a trained and experienced soldier. He thought in terms of warfare, and he believed that the only way to deal with the Indians was by a show of force. Other English, although by no means all, agreed with Standish. Inevitably, when Indians, with their lesser concern for private property rights, stole something from the English, Standish threatened vengeance, sometimes demanding that the culprit be executed. But despite a number of incidents, there was for the moment no open warfare.

But then the situation changed. By the mid-1620s English interest in the colonization of North America was growing. Settlers continued to pour into Virginia, and a scheme was got up to start another colony in Massachusetts, not far north of the little Plymouth Colony. In 1629, five ships, carrying about two hundred colonists and their families, landed at what is now the town of Salem, on Massachusetts Bay north of Boston. The next year a thousand more arrived and,

Myles Standish was added to the Mayflower company because of his skill as a soldier. He had a tendency to resort to force to solve problems and favored a tough stance toward the Indians.

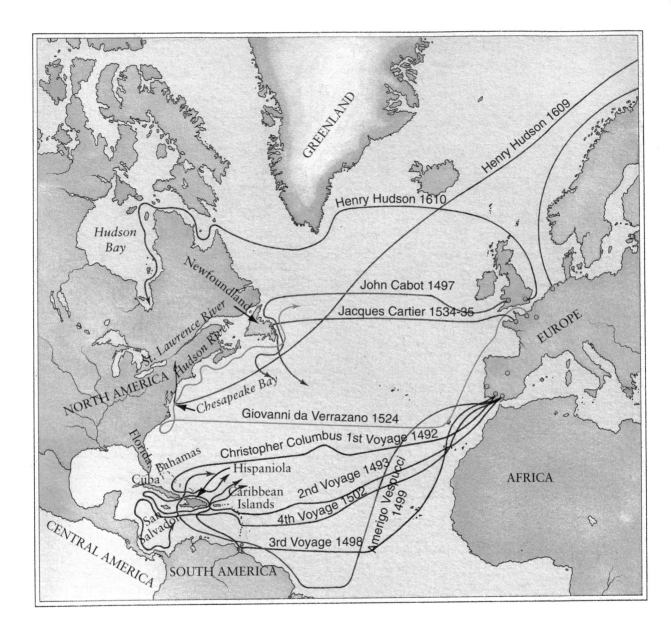

with Boston as its center, the Massachusetts Bay Colony came to over-shadow the Plymouth Colony.

This new colony of Puritans shared many of the religious ideas of the Plymouth Separatists. Like the Pilgrims, the Massachusetts Bay people intended to set up in the wilderness a religious community devoted to

God. There were differences in belief, however, and the two communities remained separate, if friendly. But the leaders of the new Massachusetts Bay Colony were aggressive in recruiting members. Because of increased religious persecution in England, continued unemployment, and other conditions, between 1630 and 1643 there was a "Great Migration" of English into the new colony.

Pressure for land inevitably grew. The Massachusetts settlers soon began to spread out into Rhode Island around Narragansett Bay, along the Connecticut River in the Hartford area, and on Long Island Sound where New Haven now stands. Trade boomed—with the Indians, among the colonies, and with London back home. By the mid-1630s it was clear that the English settlers were no longer a marginal group hanging on by their fingertips but had dug themselves deeply into the new land. There were, among the English, teenagers who had not lived anywhere else: To them, America, not England, was home.

Then in 1633 yet another epidemic of European smallpox struck. It decimated a lot of villages in eastern Massachusetts and Connecticut, this time attacking the Narragansett, who had previously been unaffected by the epidemics. The Pequot also probably suffered, though no numbers of dead are known. Desperate, surrounded by both Indian and English enemies, the Pequot began to struggle for control of their land.

Yet one more threat to the Pequot were the Dutch. From their base in what is now Manhattan at the mouth of the Hudson they were pushing trading expeditions up the Connecticut River as far as Hartford. In 1634 the Pequot killed some local Indians who were trading with the Dutch. The Dutch retaliated, killing a charismatic Pequot leader, Tatobem, and some of his warriors. The Pequot began splintering; some even went over to the hated Narragansett. The beleaguered Pequot now tried to make a treaty of peace with the Narragansett, but with no luck.

By the mid-1630s the Massachusetts Bay Colony was growing rapidly. Four thousand strong in 1634, by 1638 it would grow to eleven thousand.

Surprising as it seems, the English needed more land, especially flat, open areas with good soil, which could be found in river bottoms and places the Indians had already cleared. There was not much of this left in eastern Massachusetts. The Massachusetts colonies began looking west to the rich river-bottom land of the Connecticut River valley. In 1635 people from the Boston area established settlements in Windsor, Wethersfield, and Hartford, on the Connecticut River, and by the next year there were eight hundred English in these towns.

This was not exactly Pequot territory, but they had conquered the local tribes and claimed them as tributaries. Now they saw the land flooded with English settlers. There were skirmishes and killings on both sides. Finally, in 1637, hoping to drive the English out, the Pequot raided Wethersfield, killed nine settlers, and kidnapped two girls. The war was now on.

The English, with their strong religious bent, had concluded that Satan lived among the Pequot. We must remember that to these English the Devil was very real, and they held him responsible for a lot of the troubles the Christian settlers suffered from. It was rumored among them that the Pequot, protected by satanic magic, could not be harmed by English swords. For the English, the battle was turning into a holy war, with the Christian English pitted against the satanic Pequot.

Until the early 1630s the mighty Pequot had been overlords of much of what is now Connecticut. They desperately sought allies among the neighboring tribes, but decades of animosity between them and tribes such as the Narragansett and the Massachusett made Indian unity impossible.

The English put together a small army of some ninety men. They then persuaded the Narragansett and a Pequot splinter group, the Mohegan, to join them in an attack on their tribal enemies. The target was the principal Pequot village on the Mystic River in Connecticut. They chose to attack when the main force of Pequot warriors was away on another mis-

This woodcut, made in about 1820, gives a later artist's idea of an Indian massacre. Cruelty and needless bloodshed were frequent on both sides.

sion. The English probably only intended to take the village and plunder it, but the hundred fifty warriors who remained fought back ferociously. The English then decided to sweep the Pequot away. The Pequot, however brave, were no match for the heavily armed English and their Indian allies. The English slaughtered the Pequot indiscriminately, killing hundreds of men, women, and children, and burnt the village to the ground.

When the main Pequot armed force arrived they were so demoralized by the sight of their village in ashes and their families butchered that some two hundred of them surrendered to the Narragansett, and the rest fled. The Pequot were finished as a force; and when, about forty years later, the English would once again fight the Indians in King Philip's War, the remaining Pequot would fight with the whites.

It must be said that the wholesale butchery of women and children by the English and their allies (some of whom refused to participate when they saw what was happening and called out to the English to stop) was unusual. Neither the Indians nor the English had a tradition of killing anyone but warriors and, in general, had not done so to this point. The truth is that once hostility begins to spiral upward, turned by revenge answering vengeance, slaughter of this kind is likely to happen. It happened when the Virginia Indians massacred settler families along the James River in 1622; it happened at the Mystic River village when the English massacred the Pequot. The massacre of innocents is one of the givens of history.

CHAPTER VI

The Clash of Cultures: Winners and Losers

The victory of the English over the Pequot did not completely end Indian hopes of driving the English away. Not until King Philip's War in 1676 was the English triumph sure, and the last Indian battle in the United States was not fought until 1890. But with the defeat of the Powhatan group in Virginia and the Pequot in New England, Indian hopes of preserving their land and their precontact culture was, realistically, doomed.

Why? The Indians had begun with all the advantages. They vastly outnumbered the Europeans; they knew the territory intimately, while the Europeans did not; they were well provisioned with food and weapons, and while they did not have gunpowder, their bows and arrows were effective enough; and they had among them thousands of trained fighters with experience in battle. It is clear that if the Indians had mounted carefully planned attacks on the tiny, weak European settlements at the outset, they could easily have driven the English away. Indeed, all they really had to do was besiege the settlements, refuse the colonists food, and starve them to death. Seventeen years after the founding of Jamestown, leaders there thought that the Indians "might easily in one day have destroyed our people." Why didn't they?

The reasons are many. For one, there were the epidemics. The effect of the massive deaths due to European illness was both physical and psychological. In the 1500s, before the spread of diseases into the Virginia area, Powhatan's tribe and its allies may have included as many as one hundred thousand Indians. This would have given Powhatan a fighting force of about thirty-five thousand warriors. By the time the Jamestown settlers arrived, the Indian population was down to fourteen thousand. But the effect of the epidemics was psychological as well, for the Indians saw their people dying off in great numbers, while the English remained relatively untouched. It appeared to both sides that the English had a more powerful god, and this forced the Indians to wonder if they should simply give way.

But disease itself would not have done it, for despite the epidemics, during the first generation of European settlement the Indians still vastly outnumbered the English. An equally serious problem was the inability of the Indians to set aside old feuds and join forces against a common enemy. At first many of the Indians, such as Powhatan, did not see the tiny English settlements in their midst as a serious threat. Some, like the Indians of the beaver country to the north, wanted Europeans around so they could trade for glass beads and metal hatchets. Others like Powhatan hoped to turn English guns against their own enemies. None of them could envision the wave of English who would pour into the new land, especially in the years between 1630 and 1640, when English migration became a flood. In the end it was the English who managed to turn Indian bows against each other—the Narragansett against the Pequot, the Powhatan against the Iroquois. Had the Narragansett and the Pequot decided to clear Connecticut and Rhode Island of whites, together they could have done so. Instead, they fought each other.

Another problem for the Indians was the two cultures' different ways

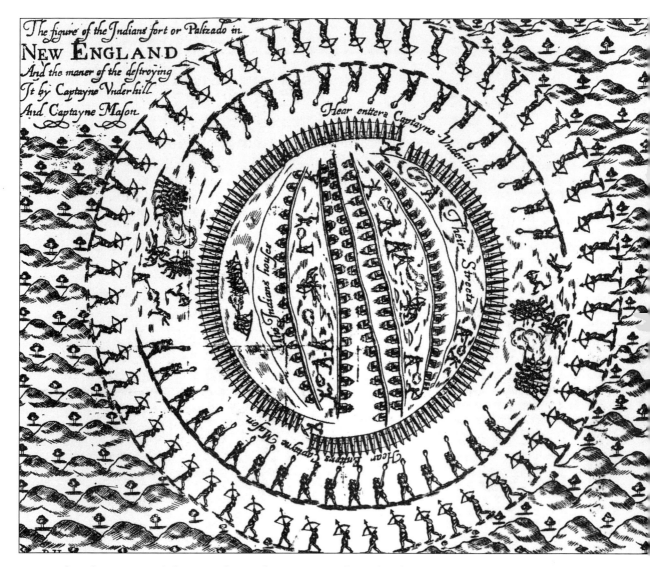

The figure of the Indians fort or Palizado in NEW ENGLAND And the maner of the destroying It by Captayne Vnderhill And Captayne Mason.

Hear enttera Captayne Vnderhill

Their Streets

The Indians houses

Hear Enttera Captayne Mason

This depiction of the attack on the Pequot village by the English and their Indian allies was published in London in 1638, shortly after the fighting ended. The Indians are shown firing arrows in the outer circle, the English with their muskets in the next circle. Inside the palisade are five rows of Indian houses, and some Englishmen and Pequots are fighting at close quarters.

of fighting. In Europe, wars were usually fought by massed armies of soldiers hired or forced to fight, who were to a considerable extent seen by their kings and princes as cannon fodder. Battles were fought until one side was clearly victorious and were usually very bloody.

Indian armies, on the other hand, usually included most of the men of the tribe. No Indian group, especially a small village, could afford to risk the loss of a considerable number of men, especially over a question of pride or injured dignity, frequently a cause of war. Battles were fought almost as athletic contests, to keep killing to a minimum. Just enough actual fighting went on to establish which side was dominant. This concept of war put the Indians at a disadvantage against the English, whose idea was to drive the enemy into submission at any cost.

A third, related problem was the differing cultural views of landowning. The aim of a chief like Powhatan was not so much to take over another tribe's land as to establish his dominance over the other group through treaty, gift giving, or war. But the English, with their system of farming, needed full possession of the land in order to let cattle graze, hogs forage, and hay and other crops grow. Where the two groups existed side by side there was always friction: English hogs devoured Indian corn and beans, and Indians routinely slaughtered English hogs they found loose; English dams interfered with Indian fishing grounds, and Indians stole whatever the English left lying around. Each side behaved according to different cultural rules. In theory a deal could have been struck. But because the English population kept increasing, their need for land was almost insatiable. And land was the one thing the Indians could not afford to give.

Finally, the Europeans were technologically considerably ahead of the Indians. The Indians were about where Europeans had been some seven thousand years earlier, in transition between a Stone Age culture and a farming one. The Europeans had firearms—frightening if not always deadly, metal swords and armor, ships capable of sailing around the world, and a system of architecture that allowed them to build not just massive cathedrals but forts impervious to Indian arrows. And though their diet was no more healthy than that of the Indians, it included domestic cattle, sheep, hogs, fowl, and a large variety of plant food.

Perhaps more important, the Europeans had developed a body of scientific knowledge that far outstripped that of the Indians. In 1600 European science was still in its beginning stages, nothing like the science we have today. Nonetheless, the Europeans had a far better understanding of the motions of the earth, the stars, the sun, and the moon than the Indians did, which among other things permitted them to navigate thousands of miles across empty seas. Indeed, their understanding of one basic fact, that the earth was a sphere, precipitated the clash of cultures to begin with.

Central to the development of this science was written language, in which knowledge could be preserved. Of course the Indians did preserve a lot of knowledge through tradition and memory, which was passed down the generations. But tradition and memory cannot hold the amount or accuracy of knowledge that can be stored in libraries full of books.

Moreover, the Indians were divided by five hundred languages and thousands of dialects, while educated Europeans all understood one language, Latin. This was critically important, for it meant that a Pole who had got hold of one part of an idea could find out about another part discovered by a Swede. More than that, through the new invention of printing, information could be spread fairly quickly. For example, knowledge of the discoveries and explorations of the New World spread around Europe within a few years via the printed word, although a good deal of the information was not very accurate. By contrast, a hundred years after Columbus, the Indians of the Northeast still had no idea of the conquest and enslavement of the Central and South American Indians by the Spanish. If they had, surely they would have been more alarmed by the arrival of Europeans on their own shores.

Beyond technology, there was a difference in *attitude* between the two cultures that proved critical. The Indians had a *conservative* culture, which inclined people to accept life as they found it. They lived in tune with their environment, extracting from the woodlands, the rivers, and the oceans what nature offered them.

The European culture was *dynamic*. Europeans did not simply accept what the environment offered. Instead, they tried to control it. They stripped the woodlands of trees and planted wheat, apple trees, and herbs. They bred cattle, horses, sheep, and goats to produce cows that gave more milk, sheep with thicker wool. They dammed streams, harnessed the wind to windmills, drained fens and swamps, built dikes to push back the seas. They were endlessly inventive, learning how to smelt copper, make the harder bronze from copper and tin, make steel from iron, and make brass from copper and zinc. They developed glass windows, printing presses, magnifying glasses, ships that could sail against the wind across vast oceans, cannons that could knock down fortresses.

We should not exaggerate the differences. Indian life was not completely unchanging. The Indians invented their agriculture on their own, developed types of corn, beans, and other plants. Some of their vegetables, like corn, potatoes, and tomatoes, were eagerly adopted by Europeans. The birch-bark canoes of the northern Indians were superior to anything of the sort the Europeans had; their bows and arrows, even with stone points, were about as good as European metal-pointed ones. Wigwams, tepees, and longhouses were more fuel efficient than European dwellings. Life for the Indians did evolve.

Conversely, the Europeans were conservative in some ways. Their religion changed very little for centuries at a stretch. Peasants, serfs who were tied to the land, often went on farming in the same fashion generation after generation.

Nonetheless, the differences in attitudes were real and important. Where change came only slowly to Indian culture, the European impulse for improvement allowed it to leap ahead of the Indian one. In the end the Europeans created a culture that—with the essential aid of European disease—simply overwhelmed the Indian way of life.

Looking back on it, we can see that what happened was inevitable, given the core beliefs of both cultures. True, if the Indians had stood together against the interlopers, they may well have fended off the Europeans for another century, or even more. But they could not have done so indefinitely. By 1600 the Europeans had developed a rich and varied system of agriculture. The surer supply of food provided by farming encouraged an increase in population. The growing population in turn required more woodland to be cleared to provide more fields and pastures which in turn encouraged even greater increases in population. By the 1600s many Europeans, especially the English, felt that their lands were getting overcrowded. Sooner or later the time would have come when they would have started looking for room to spread out. Even if there had been no gold in the Andes, no cod in the North Atlantic, no beaver in Newfoundland, the Europeans would have pressed into the Americas just to find homes for surplus people. Even by the largest estimates of pre-Columbian population, there were fewer than two Indians per square mile in North America. Europeans thought of themselves as crowded. Once they discovered what they took to be an empty land, the die was cast. Really, after 1492, there could be no turning back.

Given these conditions and attitudes, then, European dominance was inevitable. At the time many Europeans saw this and felt that it was their destiny to take over the New World. Many of them hoped it could be done peacefully, with the Indians gradually being drawn into the European culture. In this they were deluded: The Indians were no more willing to give up their ways than the Europeans were, and in the end they made a stand and fought. It was a fight they would not win.

BIBLIOGRAPHY

Many of the books that are no longer in print may still be found in school or public libraries.

For Students

Barden, Renardo. *The Discovery of America: Opposing Viewpoints.* San Diego: Greenhaven Press, 1989.

Brenner, Barbara. *If You Were There in 1492.* New York: Bradbury Press, 1991.

Calloway, Colin G. *Indians of the Northeast.* The First Americans Series. New York: Facts on File, 1991.

Faber, Harold. *The Discoverers of America.* New York: Simon and Schuster, 1992.

Murdoch, David H. *The North American Indian.* 1961. Reprint. Eyewitness Books. New York: Alfred A. Knopf, 1995.

Reader's Digest, Editors of. *Mysteries of the Ancient Americas: The New World Before Columbus.* New York: Reader's Digest Association, 1986. (Out of print.)

Sattler, Helen Roney. *The Earliest Americans,* ill. Jean Day Zalinger. New York: Clarion Books, 1993.

Wolfson, Evelyn. *From Abenaki to Zuni: A Dictionary of Native American Tribes,* ill. William Sauts Bock. New York: Walker and Company, 1988.

Wood, Marion. *Ancient America.* The Cultural Atlas for Young People Series. New York: Facts on File, 1990.

Yue, Charlotte. *Christopher Columbus: How He Did It,* illtd. David Yue. Boston: Houghton Mifflin, 1992.

For Teachers

Axtell, James. *The European and the Indian: Essays in the Ethnohistory of Colonial North America.* New York: Oxford University Press, 1982.

_____. *The Invasion Within: The Contest of Cultures in Colonial North America.* New York: Oxford University Press, 1986.

Bragdon, Kathleen J. *Native People of Southern New England, 1500–1650.* Norman, Okla.: University of Oklahoma Press, 1996.

Cave, Alfred A. *Pequot War.* Native Americans of the Northeast Series. Amherst: University of Massachusetts Press, 1996.

Crosby, Alfred V. *The Columbian Exchange: Biological and Cultural Consequences of 1492.* Westport, Conn.: Greenwood, 1972.

Grumet, Robert S. *Historic Contact: Indian People and Colonists in Today's Northeastern United States in the Sixteenth Through Eighteenth Centuries.* Norman, Okla.: University of Oklahoma Press, 1995.

Jennings, Francis. *The Invasion of America: Indians, Colonialism, and the Cant of Conquest.* Chapel Hill: University of North Carolina Press, 1975.

Kupperman, Karen Ordahl. *Settling With the Indians: The Meeting of English and Indian Cultures in America, 1580–1640.* Lanham, Md.: Rowman and Littlefield, 1980.

Rountree, Helen C. *Pocahontas's People: The Powhatan Indians of Virginia Through Four Centuries.* Norman, Okla.: University of Oklahoma Press, 1990.

Russell, Howard S. *Indian New England Before the Mayflower.* Hanover, N.H.: University Press of New England, 1980.

Salisbury, Neal. *Manitou and Providence: Indians, Europeans and the Making of New England, 1500–1643.* New York: Oxford University Press, 1982.

_____. "The Indians' Old World: Native Americans and the Coming of Europeans." *The William and Mary Quarterly.* 3d ser., no. 53 (July 1996): 435.

Trigger, Bruce G., ed. *Northeast.* Handbook of North American Indians Series. Vol. 15. Washington, D.C.: Smithsonian Institution Press, 1979.

Vaughan, Alden T. *New England Frontier: Puritans and Indians, 1620–1675.* Rev. ed. Boston: Little, Brown, 1979.

INDEX

Page numbers for illustrations are in **boldface**

JAMES LINCOLN COLLIER is the author of a number of books both for adults and for young people, including the social history *The Rise of Selfishness in America*. He is also noted for his biographies and historical studies in the field of jazz. Together with his brother, Christopher Collier, he has written a series of award-winning historical novels for children widely used in schools, including the Newbery Honor classic *My Brother Sam Is Dead*. A graduate of Hamilton College, he lives with his wife in New York City.

CHRISTOPHER COLLIER grew up in Fairfield County, Connecticut, and attended public schools there. He graduated from Clark University in Worcester, Massachusetts, and earned M.A. and Ph.D. degrees at Columbia University in New York City. After service in the Army and teaching in secondary schools for several years, Mr. Collier began teaching college in 1961. He is now Professor of History at the University of Connecticut and Connecticut State Historian. Mr. Collier has published many scholarly and popular books and articles about Connecticut and American history. With his brother, James, he is the author of nine historical novels for young adults, the best known of which is *My Brother Sam Is Dead*. He lives with his wife, Bonnie, a librarian, in Orange, Connecticut.